# HOW TO CELEBRATE
# BURNS
# NIGHT

A modern and informal guide
to celebrating Scotland's most
famous poet, Robert Burns

## By Daniel Bee

**happy**thought☺

# Foreword

How many celebrations, of any type, can bring a personal feeling of great warmth, individual and (inter)national identity and pride, have no limits as to location, size, scale and cost, have no direct religious connections and restrictions and are even flexible about date!? Unless I am wrong, Burns Night is unique in this respect.

Once the excesses of Hogmanay and New Year's Day have passed, late January belongs to a Scottish poet and songwriter, Robert Burns, who was born in 1759 and has shaped the world we know today.

Burns and his friends' recognition supper, which started in 1801, is something that I have built a very close connection to in the last 30 years of my life – in many cities, countries and even continents. It's a true moment to be with friends, family and a fantastic romantic platform for any person wishing to woo a lover (or mischievously try to woo someone else's!).

Burns Suppers have all the ingredients of traditional feasting and celebration but, two hundred and fifty or so years after he was born, the event of a Burns Supper has withstood the test of time and is flexible enough to be relevant in the modern world. If you wish, you can have a traditional Burns supper or, as I really really believe, it can be very open to a modern interpretation that you can tailor and enjoy to suit your own requirements.

This wee guide book is here to help you create your own celebration. If you are looking for a formal, academic literary introduction to the great works of Burns, I urge you to do so; but this isn't it. This is a fun re-look at a wonderful chance to bring people together.

Let me try to put this differently. In the same way that Coca Cola recently allowed you to put your name on their bottle, I think a Burns Supper can have your mark; your passion; your wishes embossed upon it. While I make mention of Coca Cola, did you know that Robert Burns was the first person to ever feature on a commemorative bottle of the rather 'bad-for-you sugary drink?' – It is somewhat ironic that Scotland's other favourite national drink. Irn Bru, did not get there first.

The overall format and the running order of a Burns Supper has remained unchanged since 1801 (more on that later), but I would say that you should not feel burdened if your event is just for two or for thirty two or even for two hundred – just set out to enjoy it. I have always thought and said about getting people together to drink and eat and recite some poems and songs… "Burns would approve."

**Daniel Bee**

# Contents

## How to celebrate Burns Night

## Order of events

## Food

## Drinks and beverages

## Burns Poems and songs

## Finishing touches

# Introduction

This book is meant to be a simple guide to hosting a fabulous Burns Night celebration. People often ask: How do I get a Burns Supper right?

**So let us get going...**

Keep it relaxed and fun. We have a suggested order of events, poems and song lyrics and even tips on how to cook the haggis. Laid out simply and designed to maximise your fun, this book can be used to celebrate Scotland and Robert Burns any night of the year!

Burns night is held on or around January 25th and every year is celebrated by millions of Scots and friends, living all around the world. It is especially popular with ex- patriots living in Canada, United States, New Zealand and mostly anywhere else that sells whisky, or plays golf.

*The baird will be happy 'yer havin a go!'*
*Raise a dram tae Rabbie Burns.*

# Robert Burns

## About the man

Robert Burns (often know as Rabbie) is Scotland's best loved writer and poet and is considered one of the most famous people in Scotland's cultural history. As a pioneer of the Romantic Movement and his lyrical poetry and songs are loved all around the world. Not only has he his own unique identity – he has, in so many ways, come to define Scotland.

He was born on January 25th, 1759 in Alloway, near Ayr, in the southwest of Scotland. His father was a struggling tenant farmer, and Burns had only a few years of formal education before family financial worries forced him to work as a farm labourer.

Whilst back on the family farm he met his first love, Nelly Kirkpatrick. She inspired him to try his hand at poetry, a song entitled 'O, once I lov'd a bonnie lass', set to the tune of a traditional reel.

When his father died in 1784, he and his brother Gilbert rented a farm near Mauchline in Ayrshire. A farmer's hard way of life taught Burns to take joy in fleeting pleasure and to be sceptical of the moral codes of the well-to-do. These attitudes, along with his capacity for love, friendship and hearty fellowship, provided the chief themes of his poetry.

Burns clearly had a way with the ladies and, in his short life, he fathered eight illegitimate children, born to five different women. One of these, Jean Armour, bore him twins and became his wife in 1788. *However some suspect there were more children than that!*

In the hope of raising some money, his first published work was 'Poems, Chiefly in the Scottish Dialect'. This collection of verse contained many of Burns best works, including 'To a Mouse', and 'The Holy Fair' and was released to much critical acclaim.

Burns had planned to escape the tough life of farming by moving to sunnier climes in the West Indies, but then buoyed by his flourishing reputation as an unschooled 'Ploughman Poet' he moved to Edinburgh and became part of the thriving cultural scene there. In a matter of weeks he was taken up by society and was transformed into a national celebrity.

However the trappings of fame did not bring fortune and he took up a job as an excise man (tax collector) to make ends meet.

While collecting taxes he continued to write, also editing a collection of Scottish folk songs, titled 'The Scots Musical Museum", to which Burns himself contributed over 150 songs, including the now famous 'Auld Lang Syne'.

In the last years of his life, Burns penned many of his great poetic masterpieces such as 'The Lea Rig', 'Tam O'Shanter' and 'A Red, Red Rose'. In 1795, he was inspired by the events of the French Revolution to write 'For a' that and a' that', his cry for human equality.

One year later, on July 21, 1796, aged 37, Burns died from rheumatic heart disease. He was buried in the churchyard of St. Michael's in Dumfries, at the same time as his wife gave birth to their ninth child.

In the decades since his death, his writings have directly inspired many. John Steinbeck – 'Of Mice and Men' which is taken from a Burns poem 'To a Mouse' which read: 'The best laid schemes o' mice an' men / Gang aft agley.' (The best laid schemes of mice and men / Often go awry).

Bob Dylan declared that the work of Burns has given him the greatest creative inspiration and it is rumoured that Michael Jackson was working with the great poet's work before his death.

And let's face it, it's the poet who tells the world when the new year starts with 'Auld Lang Syne'.

# Order of Events

There is a traditional order of events to a Burns Night Supper celebrating the life and times of Robert Burns, but depending on location, your resources and priorities for a party, do not feel that you have to follow them to the letter.

Our recommended short list for a more informal event: 'The Selkirk Grace', an 'Address to the Haggis', a Toast to the Lassies (ladies), a reply from the lassies and to end, a sing-a-long to 'Auld Lang Syne'. We feel these few are enough to get the flavour of a Burns Night celebration.

BUT the key thing that will really help make your Burns Supper run smoothly, is to prepare your guests in advance with any participation that you wish them to undertake. If there is going to be group of you, you are best to assign the key tasks of: Master of Ceremony (normally the host), the reading of the Grace, Address to the Haggis, the Immortal Memory and the two Toasts. In addition you might want to find a musician or singer who wishes to try a Burns song or other guests who are happy to read a poem.

Below is a traditional order of events at a Burns Supper celebration with further explanations of each step on the following pages.

• Piping in the guests/formal welcome

• Arrival drinks

• The Selkirk Grace

• Starter – maybe soup

• Piping in the Haggis

• Address to the Haggis & a Toast to the Haggis

• After dinner entertainment

• The Immortal Memory address

• Songs, music & readings

• Time for dessert

• A toast to the Lassies

• Reply to the toast to the lassies

• More Songs & Poems

• Closing Remarks (master of ceremonies)

• Auld Lang Syne

## Piping in the guests & a formal welcome

I am guessing that you do not have a  piper pipes on your speed dial... I know that I lost touch with the one I knew when I left school in Edinburgh, so if you have a big event you may want to hire one or download some music.

The tradition is that pipe★ music, live or recorded, plays in the arriving guests to the supper area and when everyone is ready there is a round of applause and the supper begins.

## For a formal event the chairman or Master of Ceremonies will welcome the guests.

(★Pipe music refers to Bagpipe music. The bagpipe is thought to have originated in the Middle East, near Mesopotamia and then later brought to Scotland by the by the Celtic tribes migrating from Scythia, in central Europe, though and around the coastal fringes of Europe. The Scots have made their own type of bagpipe famous but versions of similar instruments also still exist in Northern England, Ireland, Italy, Spain, France, Albania and Egypt.)

## The Selkirk Grace

This is probably one of the only religious moments that you may wish to make reference to in a Burns Supper.

This is used as the grace before the meal and was written by Robert Burns in 1787.

*Some hae meat and canna eat,*
*And some wad eat that want it,*
*But we hae meat and we can eat,*
*And sae the Lord be thankit.*

## Piping in the haggis

The haggis is the main dish of the evening and must be welcomed in style, with pipe music if possible and perhaps on a silver plate at the front of a procession of cook, piper and speech maker, plus someone with a whisky bottle to prime the pumps before the toasts are given.

Everyone claps in time to the music until everything is ready. I would recommend 'Scotland the Brave' as a good option. *Next comes the address.*

## ☙ Address to the Haggis & Toast to the Haggis

It is the big moment of the night. The haggis has arrived, a person has been selected in advance to address it and the room goes quiet.

Now, tradition has it, that you should attack all eight verses of this most beautiful poem, but I know in the past, that it is quite a big thing to ask of someone to read or memorise it, so I generally ask my guest to stick to verses one, two, three and eight.

Book in one hand, knife in the other... when you get to the beginning of verse three,

**'His knife see rustic Labour dight',**

raise your knife and then as you say:

**'an'cut you wi' ready sleight'**

CAREFULLY pierce your haggis – the next line:

**'Trenching your gushing entrails bright, Like ony ditch.'**

Put your knife down and look at your beautiful handiwork of the meal about to be served.

I always find that it is always good to add a bit of extra theatre for the last two lines of the last verse two, by slowing them right down. Take a decent break and a breath between:

**'but, if ye wish her a gratefu' prayer'**....And **'Gie her a haggis!'** being sure to come to a crescendo on the word haggis. i.e. Shout it out!

Now everyone raises a glass and shouts **'To the haggis!'** and maybe a round of applause.

## After Dinner Entertainment

At this point, it's all about the participation of those that want to get involved! It's a pretty daunting task to recite or sing something in a different language – so you will want to offer as much encouragement and support as possible for each person as they perform. Again, preparing people in advance makes for the best possible out-come.

The most popular song to attempt is 'A Red, Red Rose' – but because of all the changes in pitch it's a tough one to get right. Do have a listen to Eddi Reader version as it really is the most beautiful rendition I have heard.

## Poems, toasts, songs and addresses:

'To a Haggis' & 'Auld Lang Syne', 'A Red, Red Rose' and 'To a Mouse' & 'Ae Fond Kiss'.

## Other popular poems by Robert Burns:

'Tam O'Shanter', 'A Man's a man for a 'That', 'The Cotter's Saturday Night', 'Holy Willie's Prayer', 'Address to the Unco Guid' and 'Epistle to a Young Friend'.

# Immortal Memory address

It is now the moment for the host, or a designated speaker, to deliver the key personal speech of the night. Ideally this should be prepared in advance, but if you find yourself on the hop – you could talk about what the poetry that night has meant to you so far. Whichever is the case, be sure to have a full glass before you speak.

If you want to go all out, it can be about how Robert Burns and his works have touched your life and or how Burns is relevant today. It does not have to be long, but it should lean towards a light, more humorous approach and hopefully it will get a few of your fellow diners to think their own thoughts and feelings for Burns and his poetry.

Whatever you choose to recite, tell and share with the people around you, the thoughts should end with guests standing, glasses raised and a toast to the immortal memory of the great Robert Burns. So at least we have the ending sorted for you!

# A toast to the Lassies

At this point it is the moment to offer a very positive and respectful toast to the ladies in the room. Traditionally a man would stand up and share his views, maybe sprinkled with some of Burns' most romantic words.

Again, I really want this to be flexible as possible so it can be as short as a beautiful toast or a ten minute love letter in celebration of women around the world. here is no doubt at all that Robert Burns loved woman so it would be good to reflect that lovely tone.

# Reply to the toast to the Lassies

This too can be great if it is spontaneous and is a true and passionate reply to previous toast – however, once again, a bit of forethought will also help.

One of the best replies I ever heard was from a dear friend who had written about her single status and her desire to meet a man who could recite poetry to her. It was full of romance and dreams!

# Closing words from the Master of Ceremonies

Before people fall over drunk, go home with one another or fall asleep, it is usual to thank all guests for coming and also the people who have helped or recited poems.

This would normally be done by the Master of Ceremonies or the person who has hosted the evening.

It is also a great moment to invite people for next year or for St Andrews night in November.

# Auld Lang Syne

The traditional end to any Burns Night is the singing of 'Auld Lang Syne'. It always helps to have the correct lyrics printed out (see our Poems & Songs) for all of your guests. Usually all the guests stand in a circle (or circles) holding and then crossing hands and sing this.

A Burns Supper

# Food & Recipes

## Introduction

With most parties, food and drink play an important part in the festivities and none more so than Burns Night. There is of course the famous haggis, neeps and tatties (turnip/swede & potato) and Scotland's famous whiskies to enjoy.

We have selected a few of our favourite recipes and whiskies for a Burns Supper, but there are of course many varieties of food, drink and recipes that are suitable for a Burns Supper, so feel free to create your own menu.

# Bill O' Fare

A starter of cock-a-leekie soup, followed by the main course of haggis wi neeps an' tatties, and rounded off with a choice of two sweet puddings; Tipsy laird and or raspberry cranachan.

Traditionally a cheese board or bannocks & cheese is served with coffee.

**Bannocks & cheese consists of Scottish oatcakes that could include a selection of delicious cheeses such as:**

- Bonnet *(a goats cheese from Ayrshire)*
- Dunlop *(a soft textured Scottish cheddar)*
- Lanark Blue *(similar to Roquefort)*
- Crowdie *(a soft cheese)*
- Loch Arthur *(Galloway organic farm house cheddar)*
- Strathkinness *(a Scottish version of Gruyere)*
- Classic Scottish cheddar *(from Galloway)*

These are but a few of some selected cheeses from Scotland but similar types of cheeses will be available in your country.

Wine is usually served with the meal and generous quantities of Scottish malt whisky. See our recommended list.

If you feel that haggis alone might be a little overwhelming for your guests, you could serve haggis, neeps and tatties as a starter, with a main course of a beef dish or steak pie. If you want to be really alternative, how about some of these great Scottish treats - deliciously fatty deep fried Mars Bars, washed down with lashings of Irn Bru or the standard Scottish pub beverage, Scottish Champagne, a.k.a. Tennents Lager?

# Cock a Leekie Soup

This is a very simple seasonal soup of chicken (cock) and leeks, but you can jazz it up with extra ingredients, depending on taste and preference. Either way it is a delicious and hearty starter.

**Ingredients for four people:**

• One whole chicken / or a combination of in legs, breasts, thighs etc
• One large leek cleaned and cut into 1 inch pieces, including the green part.
• Half a cup of barley or rice *(Rice would have had to be imported into Scotland whereas barley is an indigenous crop and used originally in this recipe)*
• One carrot peeled and diced.
• Some salt and pepper to taste.

**Optional extras:**

• 2 prunes per person *(In Burns time a prune would have been an exotic and expensive import but it really does add flavour to the dish).*
• Bay leaves, parsley, and thyme are welcome alternatives.

## Preparation:

Put the chicken pieces into a saucepan and cover it completely with water. Add a quarter of the leeks, (the prunes and herbs if you are using them) bring to the boil and then simmer for 30 minutes until the chicken is falling off the bone. Take out the chicken, shred and put it to one side.

In the saucepan you now have the basis of your stock. Strain the stock into a new saucepan and add the barley. Cook with the lid on for 10 minutes. Then add the carrots and most of the rest of the chopped leeks and simmer for another 20 minutes.

If the soup tastes good now, that will do; otherwise continue boiling to reduce and improve the taste. *Add salt and pepper for seasoning.*

Just before serving add a little of the shredded chicken & the rest of the herbs and a sprinkling of the rest of the leeks to taste.

# Haggis, Neeps & Tatties

Scotland's famous national dish always causes great curiosity and intrigue – much like the country itself!

Put simply, the traditional haggis is made up from lamb, beef, oats, onions and spices and if you have ever eaten a sausage or a hamburger, be reassured that what you will be eating will, in most cases, be much more wholesome and natural. Although each butcher will have a different recipe, think... mince pie with oats that is the original boil in the bag meal.

This is an old joke which explains what is a haggis:

*Buy a sheep, sell the wool...eat the rest.*

If you wish to know all the ingredients in your haggis – ask the butcher and he will probably tell you that its sheeps 'pluck' (heart, liver and lungs), minced with onion, oatmeal, suet, spices, and salt stuffed into a natural casing – like a sausage.

My Dad has his own special accompaniment to a haggis. A tin of baked beans and a large helping of the brown sauce. Cheers faither!

# Cooking and preparing the haggis

The haggis of today will generally come to you already cooked and it's basically a matter of reheating it. What I tend to do is wrap the haggis in aluminium foil and place in a double boiler or into a baking tray that is primed with water. Do check the cooking instructions for the time it takes, for the quantity you have.

## Neeps (turnips/swedes) & tatties (potatoes)

2 to 4 whole swedes (depending on size) or a large turnip. Again alternatives can be easily be found worldwide such as sweet potatoes, parsnips and other winter root vegetables.

## 10 to 14 whole potatoes (depending on size).

Use these ingredients below for the neeps and the tatties depending on taste and diet.

• Quarter pack of unsalted butter
• Cup of cream or milk
• Salt & freshly ground pepper to taste.

## Turnips:

Chop and prepare the neeps into small cubes. Bring a pan of salted water to the boil, add the swede pieces and cook for 20-25 minutes, or until tender. Drain well, then return to the pan, add half of the butter and all of the cream and mash until smooth. Season, to taste, with salt and freshly ground black pepper. *Set aside and keep warm.*

## Potatoes:

Bring the potatoes to the boil in a separate pan of salted water, then reduce the heat and simmer for 20-25 minutes, or until tender.

Drain well, then return to the pan, add the remaining butter and mash until smooth. Season, to taste, with sea salt and freshly ground black pepper. *Set aside and keep warm.*

## Serving:

After the haggis has been cut open, serve onto plates. Spoon the neeps and tatties alongside. Eat and enjoy with a dram!

# The famous Scottish Haggis

We recommend buying a haggis from Macsweens in Edinburgh, **Scotland**. If you cannot get your hands on their fine haggis, do try your local butcher or search online.

In 1984 Macsweens also invented the modern vegetarian haggis made from various nuts, oatmeal, lentils, beans and spices and really is a great alternative and truly delicious.

In the **USA**, I have only had one successful find so far, as technically it is illegal if you import it!

http://www.scottishgourmetusa.com/product/ Hamilton-highland-haggis-in-USA/haggis-for-sale-usa

If you are in **Canada** – there are a great number of butchers that still make haggis locally.

# A BURNS SUPPER

# Raspberry Cranachan

It is a traditional dish and as it is not difficult to make, it is perfect for special occasions. This is a favourite dessert in Scotland which is famous for its raspberries, so what better than this delicious pudding to celebrate Burns Night?

If possible use Scottish raspberries, Scottish oatmeal with Scottish whisky to give your **cranachan** that extra special taste.

**Ingredients:**

- 60g of medium oatmeal
- 150g of raspberries
- 4 tablespoons of malt whisky
- 4 tablespoons of runny Scottish honey
- 600mls of double cream *(use fromage frais or other low fat alternatives if you want)*

.

## Preparation:

First make the oatmeal base. Using the oven or grill, preheat to high. Line the rack in the grill or baking pan with foil and spread the oatmeal over the foil. Toast under the grill until it starts to go brown, moving it around once or twice, until the oatmeal is golden. Set it aside to cool for about 15 minutes. You can do all this with a non-stick frying pan if you prefer. Some people add sugar to the oatmeal before toasting.

Put the cream in a bowl and whip until thick. Stir in the honey and whisky, then fold in 4 tbsp of the toasted oatmeal. Reserve a few raspberries for the decoration. Layer the remaining raspberries with the cream mixture in glass serving dishes, with raspberries at the bottom and a layer of the cream on top. Decorate each dessert with a sprinkling of the remaining 1 tbsp toasted oatmeal and the reserved raspberries.

You can prepare ahead, keeping it in the fridge for an hour or so before serving, or serve immediately. Alternatively, serve the cranachan in a large glass bowl. Delicious with shortbread biscuits!

# Tipsy Laird

**A delicious Scottish take on trifle.**

**Ingredients**:

• 300g/10oz sponge cake, halved into thick slices
• 300g/ 10 oz fresh Scottish (if possible!) raspberries, or thoroughly defrosted frozen raspberries.
• 6 tbsp whisky
• 2 cups heavy/double or whipping cream, softly whipped
• Toasted, flaked almonds or amaretti biscuits (can be used as toppings as well)

**Custard Sauce:**

• 6 egg yokes, 3 cups whole cream
• half a cup corn flour, nutmeg to taste
• 1 cup of sugar

## Preparation:

Line the bottom of the dish or glasses with the sponge cake slices. Reserve a few raspberries for decoration and layer the remaining raspberries evenly over the sponge cake. Sprinkle with the whisky.

Now to prepare the custard. Put the sugar, egg yolks, cornflour and a sprinkle of nutmeg into a bowl and mix.

In a saucepan bring the cream to the boil and pour the heated cream into the bowl. Mix and return the ingredients to the pan. Heat and mix for a further 2 minutes to cook the cornflour and spoon the custard over the whisky and sponge cake mixture. Let it cool.

When the custard is set, add a thick layer of whipped cream over the top. Decorate with raspberries and a few toasted, flaked, almonds or crushed Amaretti biscuits.

# Drinks & Beverages

## Whisky

Whisky is the usual choice at Burns Suppers, either single malts or blends. Contrary to popular belief, adding a little water to your whisky should improve rather than dilute the flavour, although some whisky drinkers may not take kindly to watering down their drams!

## Wines

Robust red wines, such as syrah, pinot noir or cabernet sauvignon, make a good accompaniment to the meal.

## Beers and soft drinks

Ales, lager, punch, Scottish fruit wines or soft drinks (perhaps Irn Bru, being Scotland's 'other national drink') are all acceptable alternatives.

# Scottish Malt Whiskies

## Glenmorangie

A Malt Whisky famous for its complexity and there are few whiskies that can boast such a range of subtle notes and flavours. Generation after generation have been making this fine malt and have passed down, their tried and tested handcrafted whisky making skills since 1843.

## Highland Park

The most northerly whisky distillery in Scotland, some Scottish commentators have called the malt the greatest all-rounder in the world of malt whiskies.

## Glenkinchie

A light, clean and fresh flavour, distinctive floral and grassy nose, with some people discovering a taste of ginger in the finish.   A whisky that can be enjoyed along side some freshly grilled sardines or delicious with a slice of parmesan cheese. This is the only whisky made in the Lowlands of Scotland.

## The Macallan

This Scotch whisky was first distilled in 1824 and is a favourite with malt whisky drinkers worldwide and is often referred to 'The Rolls-Royce of single malts'.

# Whisky Cocktails

Add a modern touch to your Burns celebrations by serving a few cocktails when your guests arrive.

## Whisky Sour

A classic cocktail, consisting of whisky, lemon, sugar and a dash of egg white. Juice the lemons and mix well into the sugar and whisky. Next take the egg whites, some ice cubes and the remaining mixture. Shake and serve.

## Rabbie's Twist

For a fresh and zesty way to enjoy whisky, try this delicious mix of whisky over ice with fresh lemon juice and topped up with apple juice for a truly refreshing cocktail

## Rob Roy

Mix blended equal amounts of Scotch whisky with Italian vermouth and a dash Angostura bitters. Shake with cracked ice, then strain into a chilled cocktail glass and garnish with a twist of lemon.

# Burns Poems & Songs

This poem was written by Burns to celebrate his appreciation of the haggis. As a result Burns and haggis have been forever linked.

**Address to a Haggis**

Fair fa' your honest, sonsie face,
Great chieftain o the puddin'-race!
Aboon them a' ye tak your place,
Painch, tripe, or thairm:
Weel are ye worthy o' a grace
As lang's my arm.

The groaning trencher there ye fill,
Your hurdies like a distant hill,
Your pin wad help to mend a mill
In time o need,
While thro your pores the dews distil
Like amber bead.

His knife see rustic Labour dight,
An cut you up wi ready slight,
Trenching your gushing entrails bright,
Like onie ditch;
And then, O what a glorious sight,
Warm-reekin, rich!

Then, horn for horn, they stretch an strive:
Deil tak the hindmost, on they drive,
Till a' their weel-swall'd kytes belyve
Are bent like drums;
The auld Guidman, maist like to rive,
'Bethankit' hums.

Is there that owre his French ragout,
Or olio that wad staw a sow,
Or fricassee wad mak her spew
Wi perfect scunner,
Looks down wi sneering, scornfu view
On sic a dinner?

Poor devil! see him owre his trash,
As feckless as a wither'd rash,
His spindle shank a guid whip-lash,
His nieve a nit;
Thro bloody flood or field to dash,
O how unfit!

But mark the Rustic, haggis-fed,
The trembling earth resounds his tread,
Clap in his walie nieve a blade,
He'll make it whissle;
An legs an arms, an heads will sned,
Like taps o thrissle.

Ye Pow'rs, wha mak mankind your care,
And dish them out their bill o fare,
Auld Scotland wants nae skinking ware
That jaups in luggies:
But, if ye wish her gratefu prayer,
Gie her a Haggis

# To a mouse

**Written by Burns after he had turned over the nest of a tiny field mouse with his plough.**

Wee, sleekit, cowran, tim'rous beastie,
O, what a panic's in thy breastie!
Thou need na start awa sae hasty,
Wi' bickering brattle!
I wad be laith to rin an' chase thee,
Wi' murd'ring pattle!

I'm truly sorry Man's dominion
Has broken Nature's social union,
An' justifies that ill opinion,
Which makes thee startle,
At me, thy poor, earth-born companion,
An' fellow-mortal!

I doubt na, whyles,
but thou may thieve;
What then? poor beastie, thou maun live!
A daimen-icker in a thrave 'S a sma' request:
I'll get a blessin wi' the lave,
An' never miss't!

Thy wee-bit housie, too, in ruin!
It's silly wa's the win's are strewin!
An' naething, now, to big a new ane,
O' foggage green!
An' bleak December's winds ensuin,
Baith snell an' keen!

Thou saw the fields laid bare an' wast,
An' weary Winter comin fast,
An' cozie here, beneath the blast,
Thou thought to dwell,
Till crash! the cruel coulter past
Out thro' thy cell.

That wee-bit heap o' leaves an' stibble,
Has cost thee monie a weary nibble!
Now thou's turn'd out, for a' thy trouble,
But house or hald.
To thole the Winter's sleety dribble,
An' cranreuch cauld!

But Mousie, thou are no thy-lane,
In proving foresight may be vain:
The best laid schemes o' Mice an' Men,
Gang aft agley,
An' lea'e us nought but grief an' pain,
For promis'd joy!

Still, thou art blest, compar'd wi' me!
The present only toucheth thee:
But Och! I backward cast my e'e,
On prospects drear!
An' forward, tho' I canna see,
I guess an' fear!

# A Red, Red Rose

**One of Burn's best know and best loved works.**

Oh my luve is like a red, red rose,
That's newly sprung in June:
Oh my luve is like the melodie,
That's sweetly play'd in tune.

As fair art thou, my bonie lass,
So deep in luve am I;
And I will luve thee still, my dear,
Till a' the seas gang dry.

Till a' the seas gang dry, my dear,
And the rocks melt wi' the sun;
And I will luve thee still, my dear,
While the sands o' life shall run.

And fare thee weel, my only luve!
And fare thee weel a while!
And I will come again, my luve,
Tho' it were ten thousand mile.

# Ae Fond Kiss

**Written in a letter to Agnes M'Lehose, (also known as 'Nancy' to her friends) in December 1791, when she left Burns, and Scotland, and followed her husband to Jamaica to try to save their marriage.**

Ae fond kiss, and then we sever;
Ae fareweel, and then forever!
Deep in heart-wrung tears I'll pledge thee,
Warring sighs and groans I'll wage thee.

Who shall say that Fortune grieves him,
While the star of hope she leaves him?
Me, nae cheerfu' twinkle lights me;
Dark despair around benights me.

I'll ne'er blame my partial fancy,
Naething could resist my Nancy;
But to see her was to love her;
Love but her, and love forever.

Had we never lov'd sae kindly,
Had we never lov'd sae blindly,
Never met—or never parted—
We had ne'er been broken-hearted.

Fare thee weel, thou first and fairest!
Fare thee weel, thou best and dearest!
Thine be ilka joy and treasure,
Peace. enjoyment, love, and pleasure!

Ae fond kiss, and then we sever;
Ae fareweel, alas, forever!
Deep in heart-wrung tears I'll pledge thee,
Warring sighs and groans I'll wage thee!

# Auld Lang Syne meaning

**The words 'Auld Lang Syne' translated from old Scottish dialect means 'Old Long Ago' and is about love and friendship in times past.**

Should auld acquaintance be forgot,
and never brought to mind ?
Should auld acquaintance be forgot,
and auld lang syne?

**Chorus**:
For auld lang syne, my jo (or my dear),
for auld lang syne,
we'll tak a cup o' kindness yet,
for auld lang syne.

And surely ye'll be your pint-stowp !
and surely I'll be mine !
And we'll tak a cup o' kindness yet,
for auld lang syne.

**Chorus:**

For auld lang syne, my jo (or my dear),
for auld lang syne,
we'll tak a cup o' kindness yet,
for auld lang syne.

We twa hae run about the braes,
and pu'd the gowans fine ;
But we've wander'd mony a weary fit,
sin auld lang syne.

**Chorus**:

For auld lang syne, my jo (or my dear),
for auld lang syne,
we'll tak a cup o' kindness yet,
for auld lang syne.

For auld lang syne, my jo (or my dear),
for auld lang syne,
we'll tak a cup o' kindness yet,
for auld lang syne.

We twa hae paidl'd i' the burn,
frae morning sun till dine ;
But seas between us braid hae roar'd
sin auld lang syne.

**Chorus:**
For auld lang syne, my jo (or my dear),
for auld lang syne,
we'll tak a cup o' kindness yet,
for auld lang syne.

And there's a hand, my trusty fiere !
and gie's a hand o' thine !
And we'll tak a right gude-willy waught,
for auld lang syne.

**Chorus:**
For auld lang syne, my jo (or my dear),
for auld lang syne,
we'll tak a cup o' kindness yet,
for auld lang syne.

# Finishing Touches

## Dress

If you are hosting this event at home then anything goes, but it is a nice idea that you and your guests wear a touch of tartan! Whether it be a tartan broach, a tartan tie, skirt, or the full tartan get up; it's entirely up to you.

If you want to go all the way, hire a kilt from local stockist or dress shop. If you have Scottish roots you may well have a tartan that represents your family name.

# Learn about the kilt

The kilt was first known as the great kilt, the breacan or belted plaid. The kilt is Highland Gaelic in origin and first appeared in the 16th century as a full-length garment whose upper half could be worn draped over the shoulder, or brought up over the head.

The philibeg or small kilt, also known as the walking kilt (similar to the modern kilt) was used by Highlander's employed in logging industries, charcoal manufacture and iron smelting.

Although nowadays, the specific pattern (or sett) of a tartan is associated with a particular clan, this is a relatively modern invention, popularised in the early nineteenth century.

# Burns Night Music

The haggis is traditionally piped in by a piper in full Highland dress. At the end of the night 'Auld Lang Syne' is sung.

After that anything goes, just keep the whisky flowing and your guests will soon be on their feet for a dance.

## TOP 6 of Scottish Bagpipe Tunes

Scotland the Brave *(for piping in the haggis)*
Angus Stewart *(a reel, for dancing)*
Major Manson *(a reel, for dancing)*
Wind that shakes that Barley *(a reel, for dancing)*
Highland Laddie *(a march)*
Bonnie Lass of Fyvie *(a march)*

# 3 musical facts about the Bard

1. 'Auld Lang Syne' is recognised by the Guinness Book of World Records as being one of the top three most popular songs in the English language.

2. American music legend Bob Dylan selected Burns' 'A Red, Red Rose' when asked for the source of his greatest creative inspiration.

3. Pop singer Michael Jackson is said to have been a big fan of Robert Burns and is reputed to have worked on an as yet unreleased album setting the Bard's poems to music.

# Some traditional Scots phrases:

**Try out these phrases on your guests!**

**Lang may yer lum reek!**
May you live long and stay well.

**Whit's fur ye'll no go by ye!**
What's meant to happen will happen.

**Skinny Malinky Longlegs!** – A tall thin person.

**Mony a mickle maks a muckle!** – Saving a small amount soon builds up to a large amount.

**Is the cat deid?** – Has the cat died? This means your trousers are a bit short – like a flag flying at half mast.

**Haud yer wheesht!** – Be quiet

**Ah dinnae ken.** – I don't know.

**It's a dreich day!** – Said in reference to the weather, when it's cold, damp and miserable.

**Black as the Earl o' Hell's waistcoat!**
Yup – looks like rainclouds again.

# Some traditional Scots terms:

**Slip these words into conversation!**

**A dram** – a glass of Scotch Whisky

**Cannae** – can't

**Whit** – what

**Fae** – from

**Smashin'** – great, fantastic

**Hame** – home

**Blether** – to have a long talk

**Bonnie lassie** – beautiful girl

*Sir Tom and Lady Marion Hunter and The Kiltwalk*
*Ross King MBE, Chantal Rickards and Daniel Bee*
*invite you to*

## The Annual Burns Bash Dinner

*at The Bungalow at Fairmont Miramar Hotel & Bungalows*

Thursday 25th January 2018
7.15pm Cocktail for 8.00pm Dinner

In support of BAFTA Los Angeles – Scottish Scholarships

Fairmont
MIRAMAR HOTEL & BUNGALOWS

THE BALVENIE

Dress code – A wee bit of tartan, or a lot

# My Burns Night celebrations

From my kitchen table to large events, Burns Night always brings together old friends and colleges.

Here are a few photos from my last event to inspire you…

Many thanks, and I dedicate this book to my mum, dad and brother for their unwavering guidance and support. The two best haggis makers in the world, Jo and James Macsween To my dear departed friend Darius Campbell Danesh – Thank you for one of the loveliest addresses to the Haggis I have ever had the pleasure of hosting.

If you have enjoyed **'How to celebrate Burns Night'** please leave us a review on Amazon.

## How to celebrate Burns Night

A modern and informal guide to celebrating
Scotland's most famous poet, Robert Burns

Daniel Bee • Happythought

ISBN: 9781507585849

Paperback

Made in the USA
Las Vegas, NV
25 January 2024

84904688R00052